Maher Asaad Baker

Vistula Resonances

ISBN Softcover: 978-3-384-38671-7

ISBN Hardback: 978-3-384-38672-4

ISBN E-Book: 978-3-384-38673-1

Cover image designed by Freepik

Contents

Introduction

Originally the musical tradition in Poland is believed to have its origin in the pre-medieval period when there existed some Slavic tribes in the territory of future Poland. These early communities consisted of people who over time cultivated a great appreciation of music and dance and used instruments like gusle – a violin with just one string and lira, a bowed lyre. Everyday activities such as work, rituals and festivities in the lives of these tribes included music. The traditions of neighboring cultures, including the Byzantine and Mongol Empires, added more colours to these kinds of music and made quite a combination.

With the development of Poland as an entity in the medieval age, the influence of the Church is seen to be more and more marking the development of music. Through monasticism, new forms of sacred music such as the Gregorian chants were introduced and incorporated into Europe's music literature. From the earliest written evidence for Polish music, it is clear that Christian influence had been significant; Bogurodzica, a hymn to the Virgin Mary.

The Renaissance means 'Melodic Awakening' in Poland, which entered the path of the European Renaissance of culture and art. At the same time, the appearance of polyphony and secular compositions came into focus, there were two Polish most famous composers Wacław z Szamotuł and Mikołaj

Gomółka. Polish Renaissance was characterized by producing elaborate and emotive music which was characteristic of the movement's intellectualism.

The Baroque period added more light to Polish music with such composers as Marcin Mielczewski as well as Grzegorz Gerwazy Gorczycki who provided Polish music with beauty as well as complexity it not had before. In this regard, one could state that the impact of Baroque music characterized by the embellishment and ornamentation and stressing the affective aspects of music has been felt in Poland through its effect on Polish composers and musicians.

The awakening of the national culture of the Poles in the era of Enlightenment was to a considerable extent influenced by music. The music of that time invited and embraced enlightenment in music by composers like Michał Kleofas Ogiński and Józef Elsner writing pieces that spoke liberating spirit of the Polish people. This means that the music of this time embodies a growing clarity of national identity, raining for romantic nationalism.

In the second half of the 19th century, romantic nationalism categorized Polish music whereby Fryderyk Chopin and Stanisław Moniuszko contributed to the music portraying the struggle and the hope of the Poles. Chopin extended the title of the world-renowned composer whose compositions contained both the forms of the European classical tradition and the motifs of Polish folk music. Some of the works that he composed include Polonaises and Mazurkas and through these pieces, he popularized and brought out the Polish culture to the world.

In the late 19th and early 20th centuries, nationalism took hold and folk influences were incorporated into the scores of this music. Second has been the following movement, which could be exemplified by the works of Karol Szymanowski and Witold Lutosławski, who, inspired by the richness of Polish folklore, have composed the sonata and many other works appealing emotionally.

Paradoxically, the interwar period was very dynamic in terms of socio-political relations in Poland and music did change. There were many talented Polish composers not only in the twentieth century but also in the previous centuries, for example, Grażyna Bacewicz, and Andrzej Panufnik who sought new forms and new techniques and the implication of such matters as culture and politics. Consequently, with the development of Polish cinema in addition to the modern media the opportunity for new forms of musical art was created, acting as a supplement to the existing culture.

World War II presented quite a tragic storyline in Poland and it reflected in Polish music and folklore of the specified time period. Despite the invasion and occupation of Poland, musicians and composers of that country showed extreme strength and utilized their works to create and spread awareness about the culture of Poland. This is true through the testimonies of the hidden concerts and secret performances that prove music to be a useful tool in resistance and culture.

After the war, Poland became a part of the Eastern bloc and was under the rule of communists and music had a dynamic existence with the new regime. It was tightly controlled by the state and also created conditions under which the opportunity was limited, but nevertheless, the talent of composers such as Witold Lutosławski and Krzysztof Penderecki helped to create interesting pieces in this period. Operating under communism, their works depicted personal struggles and emotional experiences that characterized the society's life.

The first attempts to liberalize music are traced back to the 1989 year which can be considered as the dawn of post-communist renaissance in Poland. The continuity and change in Polish music and folklore in this period is synonymous with tradition and innovation. It changed the course of its development, innovative genres appeared along with the revival of previous forms, characteristic for the growing culture of the newly regained independent Poland.

Polish music in the present day and age also remains to have a very rich depth and it is still developing with the existence of the new trends in the entire world music industry and the new generation of artists. This has especially been brought out by globalization whereby Poland today has a mixture of different styles and genres of music. From electronics to rap, from jazz to classical, traditional and present-day components are intertwined in the Polish musicians' productions, making it a rather lively and innovative musical culture.

New technologies opened new possibilities for the preservation and sharing of folklore of Poland. With the help of technology, one can record live performances of traditional music forms and present them in front of the world and also protect such crust formations for future generations. Also, through using digital media, traditional forms of music styles have embraced new forms and complexity as artists innovate on new sounds.

Moves at maintaining the Polish musical and folklore heritage while at the same time striving for innovation are documented by various activities and programs. These activities cover cultural activities such as festivals, as well as educational activities that are used in efforts to reinstate the value of Polish music in the 21st century. Examples of Malari's work are discussed, as well as examples of various preservation initiatives and contemporary interpretations of Polish music.

It is significant to point out that the history of Polish music reflects the national melodies of the Polish people's spirit and their cultural heritage. From the first and still, mysterious melodies played by the observed Slavic tribes or main singers of their education to the rich and colorful compositions and concept albums of today's artists – Polish music has followed the steps and stages of the country. The second aspect is about the beauty of Polish music on the note of melodies and rhythms but at the same time, it is about the feelings of Poles and their dreams and ideals. At the same time, examining the different periods and themes in Polish music, it becomes possible to embrace its richness and diversity, as well as to enjoy the result of the appreciation of this tradition.

Early Influences

The history of Polish music is considered a part of Polish traditions for centuries with musicians and musical instruments traced back to the earliest Slavic culture during 500 – 1000 AD. This involves the period before Poland was established as a country in 966 with Mieszko I and in this period most of the current characteristics of Poland's music were put down.

The Early Slavs who lived in the area of today's Poland in the Bronze and Iron Ages displayed successful results which included the use of musical instruments some of which were borrowed from neighbouring cultures. Chordophones: gusli – an ancient Slavic multi-stringed musical instrument; gidza – Baltic kankles; Aerophones: svirel – wooden flute; dude – bag pipe; membranophones: buben – drum. Of them the gusli occupies a special place in folklore of the Polish people due to Boyan – Slavic bard of the early historical epoch, whose songs are historical and heroic narratives of rulers and warriors.

Throughout Slavic pagan rituals and in everyday life in the time of Ancient Slavs, there were musical components. Musical instruments such as tiny clay whistles and ocarinas, buried with the dead imply that music was involved in ritual and possibly in passages related to death and the other world. Other tools that served functional purposes included the horns that were used for communication purposes during hunts, farming and wars. The rhythmic tunes of folk music accompanied circular dances where circular dance were compulsory for the carnival and other similar gatherings that were aimed at social purposes. To fully understand the notion of early Polish musical performance one has to realize that it was more framings, and participational, than compositions.

Long before Poland unified into a state and organized in the 10th century AD its music also evolved as a result of the contact with the other empires as well. The appearance of Christianity across Central Europe because of improved interaction with the Byzantine Empire brought in the musical style of Orthodox religious chant. The Byzantine choral singing secularised with Old Church Slavonic melodies infiltrated the Polish churches and royal chapels. The folk melodies of Polish got mixed up with the eastern modal scales as well as drones.

Subsequent incursions were from the East the most predominant one being from the Mongol empire that advanced west in the thirteenth century. Hence even though the Mongol influence in Poland was short-lived and very destructive it is possible to detect its presence in Polish music at least in the stocks used. In the eighteenth century, new fiddles such as the suka and the kobza came into existence and further on into an indispensable element of the repertory of today's Polish folk bands. Another instrument used and altered to become the Polish cymbały, the oriental koto zither also became fashionable. These exchanges are enough evidence that shed light on Poland as an international melting pot when it comes to culture.

Pre- Mieszko I era of Poland was centred on various early practices and instruments to build up a cube or the forerunner of versatile tradition. Folk music was active, and for people it was a core of the folk's identity and involved culture, the influence of Byzantium and Mongolian sophistically enriched the folk's musicality. The continuity of music traditions of the pre-medieval period in Poland has persisted up to the period when Poland evolved from the Slavic tribal state to the medieval Polish kingdom. The shrill harmonies of Slavic gusli, pipes and drums persisted into the nineteenth century as melodies recalling the pre-Christian autochthonous traditions as well as the meta-ethnical cultural stems tying Poland with the large Eurasiatic frame.

For those who might question the author's assertion, it is necessary to bear in mind that after the arrival of Latin Christianity to Poland in 966 AD, the Byzantine orthodox rite only gradually started to intrude the Polish religious musical practices and chanting. When the Byzantine missionaries took eastern Christianity to the land, they also introduced the chanting technique into their worshipping services. The development of Polish religious music owes much to the following key Byzantine influences: In my opinion, the indicated range of Polish religious music owes the following Byzantine impacts:

1. Orthodox Chant: Byzantine Greek Orthodox tradition monophonic melodious sound in the simple style of the melisma is said to have exercised a profound effect on Polish chant. The first cantors and the first composers of Poland were those who had accepted

Byzantine models of chants and were alienating melodies to Polish. These are all locally grown variants derived from Byzantine which forms the basis of chanting tradition in Poland.

2. Musical Notation: Besides the styles of liturgical music, the Byzantine Empire provided Polish religious music with the basic forms of the early notation system. Since the end of the 10th century AD Polish cantors began to write down their repertories of traditional chants by using the easier form of Byzantine neumatic notation. This notational system pointed at the main pitch and some of the ornaments of melodies by the symbols which look like current punctuation marks or neumes.

3. Modal System: Eight church tones which originally constituted the modality of Byzantine chant became an inextricable part of early Polish Christian melodies and harmonies. The pitches of the Polish chants in mode were third, fourth, fifth and sixth species of the octave, and the note progressions of the whole steps and half steps of the Polish chants were also similar to that of Byzantine chants. The third passionate mode and, even more, the fourth more ceremonially oriented mode was perceived as the most appealing by the audience.

4. Architectural Acoustics: To reconstruct the environment that provided the characteristic of Byzantine architecture, the Polish churches replicated the structures of the buildings they deemed to be optimal for chanting. The buildings also had architectural features and or characteristics for example, the central plan

domed structures, marble stone structures, arched vaults and orchestral mosaics, this assisted in enhancing the vibrancy of choral resonance in Poland's kolegiata and bazylika.

Consequently, the carriers of the Byzantine musicality of the East, namely liturgical repertoire, notation, modal organization, and ecclesiastical design influenced the formation of Polish Christian cultural self-appraisal. By tweaking as opposed to eradicating the Greek elements, Polish musicians created faith-based music which found ways of integrating the foreign pride with the conventional style.

The Mongol invasions of Polish territory in the early 13th century, while ultimately repelled, still left lingering impacts on Polish music that reveal key aspects of cultural exchange: The first elements of Polish music were influenced by the Mongol invasions in the early thirteenth century: Although repulsed, The Mongol impacts on Poland were therefore lasting in that specific features of musical distinctiveness in the exchange process were evident, namely that.

1. Instruments: Such short-necked lutes as kobuz were presented to them by Mongol horsemen; another instrument, a fiddle from the same area, khuuchir. Poles accepted these instruments and started to play them in their own ensembles, which included kobza lute and suka fiddle. They also picked up the delicate trapezoidal wooden psaltery, the koto and designed the rectangular hammered dulcimer that was named cymbały.

2. Performance Practices: The joyous and highly rhythmic character of the music played

by the invading Mongols appealed to the Poles given that the earlier they were limited to the chants of religious leaders only. Such persistent and complex dancelike ostinato riffs called khuuchir tug performed on fiddles and lutes in cycles were performed to the public and were absorbed into Polish traditions of folk music.

3. Hybrid Styles: Whereas the Mongol instruments in contact with Polish performers cut across Polish tunes and varieties of paeans to performances with foreign rhythm and callid decoration. Songs and dances are closely connected with the lively dynamics of khuuchir tremolos. It took a long time before the architectural style that is derived from the Polish and Mongol styles was replaced by other styles in the countryside of Poland because the folk architecture was passed from mouth to mouth.

4. Poetry and Song: In the same manner, while the Mongol armies symbolized war and destruction during the war, the blending of the cultures became the music of poetic verses. The energetic and sad folk songs were synchronized: The song «Internal exile to Switzerland »written in trochaic tetrameter and the three Mongol songs about victory and triumph with the dotted rhythm of the Mongol songs.

Embedded in this short, and hardly remembered musical dialogue happening during one of the most contentious periods in the history of humanity, there is a most compelling ethnomusicological study. For some time two cultures came together and produced resources, as music always demonstrated that no matter how a war can rip people apart, how much it can make two polar opposites meet and create harmony albeit for a little while.

The Polanie were the western Slavic tribes that occupied the Vistulan region that is, a vast part of modern-day Poland till around the 9th and 10th century AD. As one of the earliest definable ethnic groups that would coalesce into the Polish people, their traditional music exerted a seminal influence on Poland's early folk heritage: It can simply be said that as one of the first ethnic groups that would go on to become known as the Polish people, the traditional music they played was formative in shaping Poland's historical folk music.

1. Pastoral Wind Instruments: The Polanie tribes were mainly formed of nomadic and

farmers involved in pastel Chad agriculture industries and lived in the central lowland region. To accompany their rural life of grazing cattle and working fields, they played archaic folk melodies rich in thirds and fifths using instruments well-suited for outdoor use: Wooden trumpets called turas and long cylindrical flutes called floyaras had been used in those places.

2. Round Dance Songs: They appreciated the unity that existed among the migratory Polish people known as the Polanie. As part of their social practices, cycle dances known as kola are seen and call-and-response; short ditties in fourths and fifths. These were participatory enthusiasm dances that were done to foster harmony within a given group, especially during festivals.

3. Ritual Drumming Processions: The Old Slavic pagan prayers required processional rhythmic beating on a family of cylindrical one-headed tension drums known as buben. Dance drummers were moving and performing basic and repetitive co-ordinate rhythms for hours for intended shamanistic healing, forecasting and prayer dances.

4. Epic Bard Songs: They may be identified as the Guslari or the warrior bards and none can epitomise the early Polish folk music than them. Picking the tune of their instrument, the gusli, they sang great and lengthy heroic poems that depicted historical warfare, victories of tribal and royal leaders and other narratives that formed a generation's encyclopedia. These poems constitute a significant element of the special genre of the Polanie tradition which is reflected in the now widespread Polish folk songs.

In these diminished yet, archetypal sounds—the specters of shepherd flutes in the expansive pastures, the beat of spiritual drummers in the marches, the melody of communal dances, the story-telling lyrics chanted in war and valor, music of the Polanie resonates loud even in the contemporary archives of Polish musical anthropology.

During the Middle Ages in Poland, music was held in high esteem and was part and parcel of the society; it was the Roman Catholic Church and Monasteries that carried on with the tradition and development of music. Because of missionaries, Christianity came to Poland in the 10th century together with the notion of music in the Western church. During the past when the construction of monasteries, cathedrals, churches and schools was being constructed, sacred music had its own sanctum.

When Christianity arrived in Poland the Church attempted to use music to spread the Word of God as is expressed above. Recitations of prayers and chants were not only used when singing in the mass and other other ceremonies but it was also done mentally by the priests and monks while praying. Soft and delicate tunes of the Gregorian chant echoed in monastic corridors while the monastic individuals sang from six to eight times per day. This kind of a cappella singing was the major kind of sacred music that was developed and sustained by the clergy. Polish monks also created centers in which new chant books were then meticulously transcribed from the old ones. This act of musical transcription was relevant to the controlled practice of performance as well as to the preservation of melodic information in specific periods of time.

Sacred polyphony developed into another big segment of music once the cathedral schools were established in the course of the 11th and 12th centuries. As boys learned to read, write and sing in order to become priests, the new practice of polyphonic singing appeared. These boys were able to sing polyphonic acrobatic songs which included interlocking of several different lines during prayers. It remained this way and with the onset of the fifteenth century, Poland had developed its type of polyphonic music.

The church leaders also encouraged the use of music in religious dramas and prayers that used to be sung especially on the holy days. As for the Church, music left its walls and went to the streets of the village; it was more of a folk type of music then. As for instrumental ensembles and plays, they must also add more variety to the Polish music but religion was still dominant. It was in this genius cross-over of folk and liturgical music that a great preamble to the following musical revolution was set.

The Church has always left a profound imprint on music which extended far and wide, to monasteries and cathedrals as well as noble courts. Since, owing to the patronage of royal courts, people employed skilled musicians for chapels, the church music progressed even more, in terms of difficulty. In the late Middle Ages musicians were summoned from other European countries to Krakow and Warsaw so that Polish musicians could learn from them. It was this colourful musical scene that paved the way for the Renaissance musicians of

Poland including Nicolas Gomółka and Mikołaj Gomółka.

Held has stated that the basic forms of musical notation helped in the evolution of Polish music as new melodic contents and novelties in terms of playing techniques were recorded, analyzed and spread. Poland particularly took up the Western European staff notation system that includes four lines. In this manner, Polish musicians were able to secure a method through which they could accurately record and perform sacred melodies, complex polyphony and, what was notably becoming continually complex, other kinds of pieces. Formations began to learn music notations with Christianity, so probably in remote churches, monasteries, courts, and schools and for decades and hundreds of years nice psalm tones, hymns and chants could be multiplied.

These developed during the 13th century to include in its notations, some of the first time signatures, rests, clefs, accidentals, dynamics, and even some forms of expressions. Such expansion was particularly useful for notating rhythm and melodic ornaments. These marks were used by Polish musicians to indicate fairly persistent melismatic ornaments and flexible rhythms, especially in polyphonic choral works. With this notation, Polish music progressed to become more complex, masterful as well as long-lasting as time went on.

Research in musical sources has unveiled other types of fascinating Polish musical manuscripts from the Middle Ages. These are Byzantine notation which was used in Latin religious books from the 11th and 13th centuries, Early fragments of Gregorian chant, Latin liturgical dramas using music of the 12th century, the oldest Polish hymnal – gradual from Cistercian convent and richly illuminated choir books of the 15th century. These pieces of manuscripts provide a glimpse of the prosperous medieval music tradition that used to thrive in Poland.

Besides this notation information, there are a lot of written sources recording the early Polish music information. Writing by the monks revealed musical instrument purchasing, church renovations, and expanding the choir through the hiring of musicians and tutors, a testimony that these monks showed great respect for music. The will and the personal letters regarding the musical instruments and notes prove to be complementary to other documents describing this culturological context of the material, giving evidence to how deeply it is understood in the musical heritage enriched by the musical scores from a larger historical context.

The medieval musical traditions of Poland never disappeared but partly changed, leaving at least a trace. Further development of religious music from plainchant to complex polyphonic and hymnic styles made the very basis of voice tradition, always flowering and in motion.

In this varicolored medieval groundwork there came into being, unmistakably Polish forms in the folk music of court and village, and church. In this creative exchange in the field of folk music, the greater mobility of artists and performers brings further development with increased freedom. In this way, to the fore came such dances as polonaise and mazurka, which today are regarded as typical characteristics of Polish music.

It was in the middle of the 20th century that music for the Catholic Church received its re-awakening, and that was due to composer Krzysztof Penderecki, who dared boldly to absorb new directions into sacred works based on medieval chants and contemporary harmonies. There are works like St. Luke's Passion, Paradise Lost, the Polish Requiem, and others totally in direct connection with that ancient monk song of Poland. This point, doubtlessly due, comes entirely from the medieval Catholic Church: from those primitive Gregorian chants that resounded in the monasteries to the modern-day spirit of Polish music. As a matter of fact, Poland received not only that deeply rooted tradition of Western musical practices but also got a chance to provoke the development of singular local ones. That is, both a fundament and enduring influence on music for the following centuries.

From its mournful, bagpipes-like drones to the chimes of pipe organs, even mazurka dance rhythms—all join in that continuing sonic narrative begun one millennium ago.

The folk music has always been the distinctive feature of the Polish traditions and the characteristic component of the national identity. The traditional music of Poland has its beginnings in the distant past in the tribes that inhabited the territory of present-day Poland.

Before Poland was created as a united country in the 10th century AD, the people who inhabited the area in question had evolved several types of musical accompaniment related to farming and animistic beliefs. Songs sung at work were there to accompany the activities of the planters, the harvester, the threshers, spinners, and other workers. Simple tunes were sung with the same line repeated over and over to help maintain rhythm in workflow and to combat boredom. Paeans and sways were also performed for ceremonial reasons, as well as for festivals, initiation ceremonies, fertility of crops and crops, and the stars.

The Polish territories became Christianized around the year 966 with the baptism of Mieszko I, the first ruler of the Polish state; Although the adoption of Christianity led to the decline of the music that originated from pagan culture, the musical tradition of the Christian Church became part of Polish culture. The old pagan traditions merged with the new monotheistic religion and Western church modes and Latin hymns were incorporated into folk songs and thus creating the 'religious folk' genre.

For the next few centuries, more polonaise, mazurka folk tunes were incorporated into Polish repertoire in terms of melody and lyrics. Lyrical epics had been used to describe past incidents for instance wartime, rebellions and the rest of them. Lyrical songs were performed with devoted themes such as nature, love and passion. What began as mere drums and flutes advanced to fiddles, lutes, bagpipes, as well as the dulcimer. The greatest tendency among the conservatives of musical dialects was maintained along with the Polish highlanders, and the least tendency of the originality in the lowland music because of the impact of the German, Czech, and Romanian settlers in Poland.

Several key early characteristics defined the emergent genres of Polish folk: The following early pattern features describe the embryonic anthropological structure of Polish folk genres:

Bearing in mind these provisos, and with careful selection of the kinds of songs that were to be sung and how they were to be sung, singing while working was a common thing in fields, forests and rural communities, the songs that were usually sung being related to the work that was being done. Percussive rhythms accompanied planned synchronization, work that required group harmony such as hoeing, threshing, grinding grain, chopping wood or pulling fishing nets. Many of these were directly related to the work such as sowing songs which detailed the kind of seeds that were sown, and the season for sowing amongst others. Also, rhythms were relatively simple and the most frequently used harmonies included the first, fourth, fifth and sixth. Drums, flutes and fiddles were used to accompany the rhythm of the songs and voices and words were used in singing. These functional songs gradually transformed into play songs which were dance songs.

PO Checking Animals that fed on the pasture lands required shepherds to drive their cattle to graze on rough grounds of montane pastures. Vocal utterances included herding calls and jingles which included yells, whistles and utterances of fowl squawking sounds and were used to give directions. The songs sung when the bonfire was lit during the night hours dealt with ways of passing loneliness as was evidenced by rhythmical songs. Their words were so romantic and formed part of the lonely lives of shepherds while tending their flocks and herds during long summer days. This kind of highland herding tradition has caused the song dialect in Poland's mountain region.

The ritualized spiritual tradition was one of the sources that characterized the folk music of the early ages. Cyclical calendar festivals are associated with part of the agricultural produce and the changes in astronomical activity and are associated with singing and dancing and other activities that are meant to attract the attention of spirits that are to protect and provide fertility. The old zig-zagging chorus dances have remained as unaltered features of the folk feasts, and the per-Christian solstice songs became parts of the Christian agendas. If one listens to current popular songs or traditional folk songs such as

Christmas songs and spring welcome songs, one can still hear descriptions of reproduction cycles of nature. Others gave sad songs which they used to sing during the burial of deceased individuals. Instead, they were partially supplanted during the course of centuries with church music; nevertheless, the stylizations of the pagan mysteries are still brought out in many pieces of music by the Polish folk.

Two instruments that eventually became typical of traditional Polish music were pipes and fiddles. The bagpipes of goatskin arrived in Britain in the Late Middle Ages with Hunkers and possibly even before with Slavic as well as Roman armies. The loud tone and the high pitch are optimal for such purposes as enriching battle marches and village dances. From the 1700s fiddles are more or less incorporated and are still considered as the trademark of folk instruments. Physically they were diatonic having only four strings until developing into chromatic five-stringed models that resemble the modern violin. Fiddles accompanied the new dances and the songs New songs were still of higher pitch and had more complex tunes than the previously used flutes. To this date, Polish orchestras continue to be directed by the fiddles and bagpipes.

The early content of folk thematic and the instruments, and widespread regional dialect had a big impact. The highlanders of the Carpathian mountains however retained the most basic musical form and stuck with their vocal harmonies supplemented with the historical Romanian instruments like flutes, alpine horns, and even the bullock's bladder drums from the Dacians. This was according to what else those Highland herdsmen directly referred to it as. Because of the interaction with outlay cultures, the lowlands graciously incorporated musical developments with interaction. Commercial centers of the eighteenth century stood ready to accept foreign guitars, lute derivatives, dulcimers, Jewish harps, and mandolins. Highland music enjoined more probably regularity than the Lowlands' mobile, fluent music which could include tempo and ornate playing. This opposition of mountain and valley people established two poles wherein traditional styles could be collected from out Poland.

Polish folk naturally absorbed flavors from migrating minority cultures through its history, generating fusion varieties: Polish folk over time thusly inevitably picked up notes from the immigrating minority peoples producing fusion stocks here:

Some of them, the first Germans set foot on Slavic territories in the 13th century, while others began a large-scale migration to the Baltic Sea coast and Silesia in the early seventeenth century. This inflow has left an unmixed and tremendous musical influence on the folk songs and musical instruments of that area. Thus, some borrowed from German string and wind orchestras, which became Polish entertainment. Vocal yodeling songs and rejection, and hardship songs are the particular types that have emerged from Silesian culture. Through the same popular German beerhouse bands began using the brass sections including tubas, the trombone, trumpets and saxophones. These extended considerably the range of instrumental colour available to Polish composers.

Some of the other contributors include Jewish Klezmer music which was brought to Poland by Ashkenazi Jews who began to settle in this region in the mid 1400s. The Klezmer developed the traditional Jewish more complex with minor keys, off-beat rhythms, and melismatic vocals and in Aeolian mode went as far as Jewish-spirited wedding bands and leisure-time institutions in the Polish folk dance floors. It is necessary to note that Polish folk songs used such bouncy dashed rhythms, mournful cries and exotic scales. into their style of play, they used scooping of notes up to the proper pitch that is associated with Klezmer music.

More features came from districts of Poland which at one time or another were annexed by such neighbors as Prussia, Russia, Austria and Bohemia. They, their occupying musicians incorporated the stylistic into the

Polish lowlands perimeter. The Syncopated Bohemian and the Moravian dance pieces were also brought in as were the triple Meter rhythms associated with the Russian orthodox church in the East. Through the Prussian military horn bands, playing as well as parade rhythmics were systematically adopted. This influence affected further musicianship and orderly work that was being incorporated into folklore in Poland in the nineteenth-century stage performances. Polish folk music thus grew in the form of a mosaic of assimilation of the soils of other realms into the Polish realm.

Those who did not lose their land to aristocratic encroachment in Late 1800s Canada, incorporated their nationalist folk dances into new North American roots music that would echo back to Europe to help Poles reconstruct a folk identity after the Second

World War. They have paved their conduits; both continents are earmarked.

The battle for Polish national music started in the 19th century when the Poles started fighting for Poland in the face of their enemies-Prussia Austria and Russia. Thus, nationalist composers collected and assembled the consonant folk repertoire with the consonant-dependent court music into the patriotic suites in response to cultural substitution under hammer organization measures. Developing from jovial drinking songs and family tune books, there appeared a more systematic method from ethnomusicologists of collecting repertoire for orchestral ensembles of Polish.

One of the most extensive was organized in 1857 and has been by the composer as well as activist Oskar Kolberg. Kolberg traveled for about fifty years through the Polish countryside recording over 10,000 ethnographic folk melodies in musical notation. This anthology retained basic anthems against the feared syncretism that was feared by many. It also provided sheet music of wild harvested works for polished folk songs so that professional musicians were able to access these. Some great folk songs and not to mention words of folk which brought the minstrels and then the substance that was useful in fortifying the growth or what could be named as the formation of Polish classical music. Written ones made it possible for cafes and theaters to embellish the folk songs suitable for the newly emerging middle-class urbanites and link them with their peasants' origins.

The first Polish music conservatories also participated in the process of folk stylistic rarefaction Indeed, the Warsaw Music Conservatory was founded in 1810 and the Krakow Music Conservatory in 1888 partially out of patriotic needs to protect Polish music which was suppressed under Russian and Prussian occupations, these institutions taught Tatra highland melodies, lowland dance reels, Jewish Freilach strains, and central plain ballads as examples to classical composers. Before, military bands and bugle calls were of Moravian and Bohemian brass type and these were used for new patriotic marches. Karol Kurpinski the founder of the conservatory chose simple mazurka and kujawiak and put them into style suites that could be danced in concert halls in foreign countries to spread the Polish identity out. Lyrics of folk poets Adam Mickiewicz and Juliusz Słowacki provided a rather good source of materials to enact in dramatic programmatic tone poems that depicted Polish landscapes. The same can be said about national operas where allusions to folk songs worked as primordial sources of Polish Romanticism. This meant that Polish folk gems were admitted into the European family on merit alongside the Western forms of institutionalized music.

And that in music Polish pride was allowed full reign with none other than Frederic Chopin, the most popular pianist and composer who was French-born but adored the Polish spirit in the folk. The evidence of this is the dance precedent left by Kurpinski, which heralded the creation of hundreds of mazurkas in a Chopinesque manner and the motifs and feelings they embodied were bright, light and delicate. As the concert hall approved harmonic chromaticism and contrapuntal delicateness they chopped these with folk song cadences. The mazurkas for solo piano comprised a somber, sorrowing sort of nostalgia that recalled the terrain of occupied Poland. These bagatelles have transcended from the margins of Polish boor and Polish noble's salon to the chimeras of the suffering nation's pride and aesthetics.

Thanks to the efforts of numerous preservationists of the 19th century, Polish folk music not only survived two world calamities but also got a restart. Kolberg's archives remained unscathed by WWII Nazi destructions as sacred national assets. The artists after the war went back to folk figures in search of the stability that art can offer as well as the pattern on how to reconstruct culture out of shattered lives and societies.

Warsaw Pikadora and Krakow's Piwnica Pod Baranami cabarets featured young performers who incorporated folk influences with prewar motifs into new creative combinations. They saved such small village instruments as suka biłgorajską and lira korbowa for house bands and invited older regional folk musicians to play with the young and teach them. Folk music was allowed on the radio when stations were given requests for beloved nostalgia. These conduits prompted a root awakening and return to the nation's guttural national heritage of Poland.

Poland's very own communist regime patronized institutional folk groups as representative of the proletariat peasant class their political system claimed to be for. The official state-sponsored professional mazurka dance ensembles such as Slask or Piec Gwiazd Mazowsza toured the world showcasing an elegant sterilized vision of Polish life as pastoral romance through performance. Whereas folk music was somewhat limited in its role as a vehicle for party propaganda, the very language inherently poetic, managed to inspire the nation beyond the confines of censorship. Folk tunes thus remained an essential part of the Polish consciousness through Sea Shanties, Christmas carols and heroic saber dance overtures.

These artists, young postwar experimentists wishing to transpose folk idiom with such foreign modes as American jazz, French musette or blues-based rock discovered rich feed in archives of villages. The sources were people seeds and thus grounded their thrilling syntheses. "Yass" Polish jazz gained infamy by supporting folk fiddling with swinging rhythms, walking bass, and angular sax runs right out of the Coltrane playbook. In rock, fascination with contemporary society was connected with the romantic vision of the ancient Slavs in such bands as Breakout, Bractwo Kurkowe 17, and Klan, which used heavy guitar distortion and incorporated such instruments as Highlander flutes, shepherd horns, and shamanistic lyrics. This common impulse of hybridization entwined the DNA of Polish folk with the threads of the early development of several different genres.

And as ever the lowland-highland split persists in polarizing views on tradition as the mountain conservatives transcribe rituals through mimicry while the lowland postmodernists filter fragments through analysis. Nonetheless, despite dialectic differences, all appreciate the brilliant Polish folk wisdom that passes soul through generations.

Starting from pre-Christian times that brought Poles and their music precursors, Olędrzy, through the centuries of wars, dissolution and revival of the Polish nation's spirit multiple times over, the nation's ancient folk music continues to shine as one of the most valuable cultural assets. Many thanks to the ethnomusicologists, composers, poets, and paramilitary guards who contributed to the preservation and documentation of Poland's folk music collection as a means of escaping the historical vandalism of the erasure period. More than a thousand years of Polish symbolic music echoing back to pagan periods through Catholic assimilation, Protestant Reformation struggles, Csarist subjugation, Prussian partition, Nazi conquest, and Soviet reflections - countess external influences have been imposed over the Polish folk tradition without eclipsing its spirit. The song and dance, the elegance and the poetry inherent to the Polish country soul still thrive as an eternal flame that is sacred and promises to remain loyal to the land and its people.

Flourishing Traditions

The Renaissance period which was between 1300 and 1600 was a period of revival in many fields of human activity including art, science and philosophy. This awakening also had an impact on music production to change in a very drastic manner and open for new styles, new techniques and new possibilities. Consequently, Poland, which had quite a colourful culture, could not remain indifferent to this harmonic awakening.

Before renaissance period the Polish music was mostly of monophonic chants or singing which was part of church services. Nevertheless, it was in the context of the newly developing Renaissance style that polyphonic music – the music with several interdependent and simultaneously performing melodic lines appeared. As the cultural relations between Poland and other European countries including Italy and France grew, Polish composers also incorporated the use of polyphonic mode in their compositions.

Among them, the most famed polyphonic composer was known as the Father of Polish Polyphony, Mikolaj Gomolka who used to study at the Italian academy in Venice, the creator of the Venetian school of polychoral music Adrian Willaert. This he did later when he returned to Poland, brought in the polyphonic techniques and composed polyphonic Polish pieces for voices 4–6. He wrote a number of a cappella choral pieces with Polish lyrics which are still in practice today.

Another composer was Mikolaj Zieleński who also went further with the polyphonic style in the early seventeenth century. As is the case with Gomolka, Zieleński also began to travel to Europe to pick up new ideas and became equally popular as an individual composer. He also wrote about 500 motets and pieces of instrumental in the Polish-Italian style, which is said today to contain some of the best Renaissance polyphonic music in Europe. This work justifiably titled Communiones totius anni (Communions for the Entire Year) was a series of polyphonic pieces that were employed in the Polish churches for more than two centuries.

Not only was there the sacred music, but the development of the secular during what was referred to as the Renaissance period of Poland as well. The court musician composed and performed dance music, songs as well as vocal music for the nobility and kings. The leading court musical formation was capella which comprised of between 4 and 6 singers with several musicians. Capellas sang during weddings and funerals, religious festivals, birthdays, and any other important occasion that may demand music. As for the specifics of how proper court Capellas and as to how should be performed for Polish nobility; this was documented in detail by Łukasz Górnicki in his manual titled Dworzanin Polski (The Polish Courtier).

Therefore, the Renaissance helped in forming new tendencies in both sacred and secular Polish music. Polyphony and contact with other cultures supported and gradually developed Polish music into a special and developing genre. These gave key basics that composers have followed for many years to come as we shall see from the history of music.

The Baroque period was roughly from 1600 to 1750 and is considered to have had many advancements in music throughout Europe. Poland also underwent a style change quite conspicuously that one is called the Polish Baroque.

During the later phase of the Renaissance period and the onset of the Baroque period, Polish music adopted some of the characteristics of the new style: gilding and combination of staccato and legato, and the desire to stir desire in people. Polish composers also borrowed ideas from the Italian and later from French Baroque composers such as Claudio Monteverdi, Arcangelo Corelli, Jean-Baptiste Lully and François Couperin.

On the same note, Poland had political stability and economic prosperity during the reign of the Vasa dynasty that promoted arts and music. The Polish nobility which aimed to follow other European courts easily arranged musicians and bands. This wealth gave the circumstances for numerous production of pieces from Polish Baroque composers.

Among them was Adam Jarzębski who was referred to as the "Polish Handel" For his musical education, he took time in other countries and adopted the Italian music of the period. He returned to Poland, where he was the choirmaster of the royal chapel to King Wladslaw IV, and wrote sumptuously adorned instruments and chamber music for the royal court. He wrote concerto grossos; sonatas, masses, motets and other compositions which incorporated Polish lyrics together with Italian and French Baroque. Some of them are as follows: the most famous one among them was the Missa Purificaione Beate Virginis Mariae in A for choir, soloists and orchestra.

Another composer from the Baroque period that is worth to be mentioned was Bartłomiej Pękiel. Born as a folk musician and later he toured Poland to create regional music which he incorporated into his music. Pękiel, having settled in Warsaw under the protection of King Jan III Sobieski, used Polish folk's inspiration in Baroque style in his works. He is accoladed for his creation of more than 500 songs and instrumental compositions of masses, motets, madrigals, and Sonata Polonoica. loved and appreciated both in Poland and other countries Pękiel became one of the first native Polish composers.

Concerts were another significant feature of the Polish Baroque period as well as the accent on the opera. From the middle of the seventeenth century, Italian operas were performed quite often by the Polish nobility who appreciated such spectacles and how they were staged. It, in time, led to native Polish opera. The first opera in Poland was done in an opera titled Zielona góra (Green Mountain) by Wojciech Dankowski in 1628. In the next one hundred years over fifty more Polish operas were composed as this new type of music developed. However, even though today people do not remember these attempts, they are important in the introduction of opera in Poland.

Consequently, polish music adopted the characteristics of the baroque, but the national element could still be recognized. Nevertheless, Polish composers succeeded in producing pieces that could be recognized as Polish though they were composed conforming with European penchant at the time. It was therefore monumental in the process of constructing a national Polish compositional style of the Polish Baroque period.

Enlightenment was the movement that started in Europe in the 18th century as an intellectual pursuit of truths in the forms of knowledge and science. Once more, as it was previously with the earlier periods, the principles of the Enlightenment determined the development of Polish arts and music to a significant extent.

The most important conceptions of Polish Enlightenment philosophy had been pragmatic education, philosophical attitude, tolerance and social transformation. Thus, music and arts in liberal education were not being assessed as romantic but as rational or, in other words, not emotionally but logically. Similarly to what was taking place in the literature of the Enlightenment, composers were looking for balance, order, logic, clear lines and forms, motives and textures, and neoclassical themes that reflected the spirit of rationality, discipline, and tastefulness.

Of all the composers that belonged to the Polish Enlightenment period, Jan Dawid Holland was one of the most efficient. He was born in Holland and had a progressive education; he could play various instruments, studied enlightenment and had non-musical interests in both mathematics and acoustics which led to the well-built Holland compositions. Having returned to Poland, Holland was already conducting the opera theatres in Warsaw simultaneously with the vocal-instrumental pieces imitating the Polish Enlightenment as well as the French/Italian.

There is also another Polish composer of the middle of the nineteenth century who joined the idea of the Enlightenment, Stanisław Moniuszko. Studying composition, Moniuszko got acquainted with the concepts of the Enlightenment music theorists, including J.J. Rousseau; the main thesis was the ability of music to affect the feelings of the people and, therefore, transform society. He, therefore, had certain textual things and feelings in his writing of operas and songs and set music in accordance with rationally conceived dramatic notions. Thus, the opera Halka or Songs of Our Land are several piano compositions or choral pieces – the extra- music and outlook to folk and national culture.

The Polish Enlightenment also provided the foundation for the formation of an entirely new genre of music: from these dances, one can show an example in the polonaise. For example, developing from the regal dance of the triple measure coming from Poland, the polonaise was altered to stately instrumental music in the late Baroque/Enlightenment Age. The polonaises accordingly had refined elegant and gentlemen-like attributes as far as pace and time signatures were concerned, and as with the amenities they inculcated ethical moral lessons in the fashion of enlightenment.

Later the polonaise was taken by Frédéric Chopin and turned into a proper characteristic of Polish people. Developing from earlier polonaise composers such as Michał Kleofas Ogiński, Chopin credited the complex developed pianistically polonaise to the field of Polish patriotism including the fight against oppression from outside. In works like Polonaise in A-flat major, Op. 53 he encapsulated the impervious, enlightened Polish character inside the form of polonaise.

Hence, it can be inferred Polish music of score, performance, and philosophy during 1700-1800 had been influenced by the productive Enlightenment reason. Thus, from absolute notes to measured inhuman drama, Polish artists produced pieces that depicted the Enlightenment.

The Baroque period which was from 1600 to 1750 was very vibrant in the development of music in Europe. Continuing from the relatively more mundane-sounding Renaissance style, baroque music was just as, if not more decorational as it was ornamental. Same as the other countries with a deep historical relation to the WESTERN civilization, Poland could not stay indifferent to this shift in art direction. As the Baroque melodies were popularised, several composers and musicians from Poland also adopted the sound features of Baroque in their compositions. Even if the schools in Poland were not as developed as in Italy or schools in Germany, the latter country has established a tradition in Baroque music with several outstanding personalities. Thus the general knowledge of Poland's Baroque period can be developed further by looking into the lives and compositions of particular composers such as Adam Jarzębski, Marcin Mielczewski, and Henryk Wieniawski.

In terms of the volume of extant works, the first undisputed representative of Polish Baroque music can be considered Adam Jarzębski (c. 1590–1648). He was born around 1590 and at a young age he sang in the royal chapel choir there he outlined his musical talents. He further developed it during his musical education in Italy at the beginning of the 17 century and after that returned to Krakow as the maestro di cappella where he stayed until his death in 1628. Jarzębski's two main publications of music are entitled Canzoni e Concerti from 162758 and the Culminacione del perfetto musico from 1648, and both are examples of the Italianization process of Polish music. Out of all these pieces, it has 31 sacred vocal compositions known as 'Canzoni e concerti.' On the other hand, Culminacione del perfetto musico offers 23 motets and masses which are derived from the new Baroque attitude towards the vivid gestural representation of passions in sacred music. Altogether these works of Jarzębski can be regarded as transitional from the Polish Renaissance style to the initial stage of Baroque in Poland.

Marcin Mielczewski (c. 1600 – 1651) was Poland's outstanding composer of the 17th century. Although he was baptized in Lublin he was the director of the chapel of Sigismund III Vasa and the maestro di cappella of the Wawel Cathedral in Cracow. Mielczewskis's activity embraces all spheres of music both sacred and secular in all genres to the existing in the period motets hymns magnificats and polyphonic masses. His motet O Rex Gloriae written in 1629, makes it possible for the author to be associated with the Concertato style of Italy, he used contrasting groups of voices and instruments in his composition. At the same time, his three mass cycles guitars all together in a polyphonic manner and to it passion for new the baroque style is added. However, placing himself in the Renaissance technique, in his musica Mielczewski coined some modern traits which influenced subsequent Polish composers. He passed away at the age of 51, whereas the position of the royal director of music was then taken by Marco Scacchi, an Italian – this is yet another evidence of the baroque's firm grounding in Poland.

Moving to the nineteenth century one finds another eminent outstanding figure in violin virtuosos in the name of Henryk Wieniawski, 1835-1880. Wieniawski had a Polish mother and Jewish father and he was born in Poland. He learned music at an early age and later on received his training from a master violinist named Massart in Paris. Consequently, for his genuine virtuosity, explicitly feeling the music, brilliant performance as a soloist, and, at the same time, conducting the best musical collectives of polka, he was idolized on stages and in European music salons. But even in the tour life of an artist, Wieniawsky came up with two splendid concert pieces for a violin to enhance the fame of his name. More so, The Concerto No. 2 in D Minor is said to have become probably the most performed violin work in 1862. Packed with technical marvels and rooted in Romanticism, it is a piece with which today's stars can show that they are capable of dealing. Thus, the former success was followed by the highly desired position of a professor at St. Petersburg Conservatory during which the composer managed to influence several generations of bright Russian violinists. Performing, and teaching with his etudes and caprices, Wieniawski carried 19th-century violin music to a degree few could, and many with ambition can think of matching with Wieniawski. In later years Vieuxtemps, Sarasate, and Ysaÿe were to continue the tradition, but the laurels of the Franco-Belgian school and the formation of the personality of the Polish school on the foreign scene were to be earned by Wieniawski.

Besides the contributors themselves, it is also effective to consider the measurement of the Baroque impact on Poland encompassing the institutions which have been engaged in the evolution of the field up to the present day. Among them, one should distinguish the Academy of Music in Krakow that was established in 1888 and aimed at training musicians in Polish music as well as the European tradition. Having evolved from the Krakow Music Society and Musical Institute, it has separate, reasonably well-formed departments of performance, theory, and education from the day of its formation. Today, it prolongs it by organizing international early music festivals, particularly focusing on the collection of Polish Baroque music. Likewise, the earliest university in Poland established in 1364, Jagiellonian University, also possesses an Institute of Musicology to research Polish music. It has also played a very vital role in the present knowledge of the developments of the Polish Baroque through its research work and documented literature. It has projects such as the treasury of early music, where it tries to make scores and documents accessible to scholars and performers across the world. It is for that reason that today, when composers like Jarzębski and Mielczewski are long gone, institutions such as the Jarosław Kozakiewicz Foundation encourage today Polish Baroque music.

Starting with the climax of Adam Jarzębski, passing through the showy violin performances of Henryk Wieniawski up to the contemporary learning at the Jagiellonian University, one finds rich materials on the Polish Baroque. The principal fundamental of the ethnic Poles music was localized by the influences of the Italians and other European cultural trends. The result of this was a national Baroque sound that evolved from an apparently flexible imported aesthetic but was accompanied by ongoing domestic pressures and requirements. As the intricate stuccowork which forms so much of the Baroque art and decoration this subtle combination worked to generate something new but beautiful. Thanks to these performers from the seventeenth and eighteenth centuries they hand over to the early music revival of the present day more delicious sets that the world keeps stumbling across in the discard bin of tomorrow. Therefore, even though the names Jarzębski, Mielczewski or Wieniawski are perhaps not as well-known as Vivaldi or Bach such works should by all means be enjoyable by audiences everywhere in search for the lost gems of the baroque period. Thanks to the academic focus and performers' work, new days are opened for the Polish Baroque compositions to be enlightened.

The Enlightenment was an Intellectual and philosophical era, that was established in the early 17th and 18th centuries in western Europe. He emphasized the use of reason, science and the availability of information as some of the means the society's advancement. When these European ideas of enlightenment reached the East it was welcomed by the emerging Polish nationalism and impacted what was later seen as a strong nationalistic feeling.

By the middle of the seventeenth century, the Polish-Lithuanian Commonwealth had been experiencing a decline: the state had lost territories, and internal politics was becoming sick. But when the enlightenment ideas from Western Europe reached Poland in the early to mid-eighteenth century, liberal Polish intelligentsia seized the opportunity. It is very important to emphasize that if only the Polish society was to apply reason and throw away prejudice it might not only improve but change for the better Poland as well as the whole of humanity.

To the artists, the Enlightenment principles provided them with a reason and a purpose for producing art that would have a positive impact on society. When Polish identity was being provoked by threats of outside forces, musicians added patriotism to intricate and advanced works to sell Polish artistry all over the world. European Enlightenment principles of universalism had arrived only to discover that they had encountered Poland's core and were retranslated through Poland's specific point of view.

In the middle of the 18th century, Poland had a problem staying an independent country and thus music played a crucial role in maintaining a formation of national identity and representing the people.

People were angered after the First Partition of Poland in 1772 and the partitions themselves triggered various forms of activism in writing, poetry, music drama and more all of which contained traces of patriotism. The second component to the music becoming expressive, composers began tossing in themes that embodied the Polish culture. Such an airing out of grievances Through artworks was in harmony with the Enlightenment ideal of art as social transformation.

It was impossible not to find a place in The Garden of the Public Perverts less poignant than Witkinesque and contributing to a manner in which patriotic feeling could swiftly develop in cultivated music: After all, the birth of the Polish nationalists opera with Jan Stefani did aid this. Nevertheless, when Poland struck from the maps in 1795, nationalist music was in many respects to assist in maintaining at least the consciousness of the nation in geographical areas of art and performances.

In addition, the representatives of music were intentionally concerned with the Polish national style to bring the characteristics of Polish refinement to music and the spirit of Polish music. They created stylistic developments that reflect the constantly developing entanglement of Polish and Western European classicism of the Enlightenment.

What the West admired as certain stylistic patterns like the German symphonic form or the Italian operatic style, Polish composers used and incorporated into their works and were strongly influenced by Polish stylistic properties. Opera in Poland, begun with Jan Stefani, was further developed by Michał Kleofas Ogiński and Karol Kurpiński and they provided the infrastructural basis for a new kind of opera which can be termed as entirely Polish. Some, such as Karol Lipiński made pieces with Polish violin concertos while the violin concerto idiom was symbolic of Germanic symphonic music culture.

The creativity in this music brought out the Enlightenment ideal of creativity and Poles contributed markedly to this by the Hungarian-born Franz Liszt propounded Polish music as being 'more music than other nations.

Of course, no more appropriate person was able to epitomize Poland's journey through music during this enlightened age than Chopin. Applying mastery in music, a very high level of creativity as well as the characteristic of mazurka dance Chopin released an almost solitary vision of Polish music to an entirely new level. He thus played compositions of an international character that were distinctly Polish, thereby bringing to life through him, Polish music as a living entity on the global stage and still keeping the idea of Polish existence where there was no Poland.

While all of the fine arts, visual arts, poetry and drama served their role, music's message of unity and cohesion let its more specific, abstract content create a coherent vision of Polish nationalistic spirit across contexts. Between fanciful mazurka and solemn polonaise dances, piano-orientated compositions, and philosophical masterpieces of the romantic period, this Pole was voicing the very existence of Poland in moments in which echoes of this nation were scarce in Europe.

Therefore, in Chopin and the 19th-century sources to which I have been referring, Polish music assumes the mission of maintaining the national tradition in the course of the processes of dismantlement of the Polish state. The universalist enrichment embodied in such transcendent works reflected the duality of Poland's musical journey: developing to the cultured rationalism of the European Enlightenment while in terms of style finding support in patriotism during the period of the low statehood of Poland.

The purpose of music for creating the Polish national image is hence huge and is not only limited to the Polish arts but also raising the figure for a long-term nationalist effort.

It wasn't long until decades after Chopin's demise a pianist by the name of Arthur

Rubinstein emerged to reintroduce the European audience to the Polish music revolution that Chopin had established. Many of the 20th-century dramatic developments of this new Polish avant-garde classical presented by Witold Lutosławski and others belonged to their national form as well.

Finally, when the political movement of Solidarity made the Polish national identity alive at the close of the twentieth century, movement anthems again returned to the classicism of the Enlightenment era to sustain the solid Polish self.

He would build the connection between Polish Music and the progress in arts and culture on the international level by presenting Chopin's mazurkas as a part of the Masterpiece of the Oral and Intangible Heritage of Humanity.

Thus, despite the Polish state's internal upheavals during the two centuries following the Enlightenment, the concept of 'Polishness' has remained abroad through music. Music is thus still associated with the Polish nation's identity with which it was intertwined when constructing the Age of Enlightenment. Still, more of them remain to nourish pride and awareness of the nation and its identity through a process of creativity and humane beauty.

Nationalism's Rise

As it was mentioned earlier, the 19th century can be considered a breakthrough in the development of the music history of Poland. As the country was invaded and partitioned by the foreign power music became the only means to express Polish culture and emerging nationalism. They included in their tone painted aspects of Polish nationality, suffering, hard work and patriotism within the harmonic language, orchestration and narrative of this Romantic period. Among them, one can distinguish none as encompassing this musical representation of nationalism better than the 'Polish lion', namely Fryderyk Chopin.

Music nationalism is a relatively young ideology that started in the middle of the 19th century and gradually turned into a movement that supported Polish culture.

The late 18th century and the early 19th century may be characterized as the age of transition and chaos in Poland. The once opulent and mighty Polish Lithuanian commonwealth lost its greatness, its political instability problems and neighbors like Russia, Prussia and Austria eyeing the area to take over it. In fact, during the division that occurred in the years 1772, 1782, 1793 and especially 1795, Poland had been almost entirely dismembered. Such problems stirred up nationalist sentiments among the people of Poland to the highest level.

During this period arts were probably among the most powerful ways of voicing an opposition and asserting cultural presence when violent resistance was impossible. The free-thinking Adam Mickiewicz created marvelous epics and verses full of Polish legends, legends and the Jews' dream for the redemption of an independent country. Some painters painted patriotic scenes and some painted architecture. while composers included Polish dance motifs, sad colours, and passion owing to the fight and struggle of Poles.

This was an outstanding patriotic performance that was in harmony with progressive music and politics that was raging in Europe – musical romanticism. Romantism appeared at the turn of the late 18th and the nineteenth century and was characterized by individualism, passion, nature and free creativity. These sensibilities made their way to the national music styles as was embraced by the composers. The style that was formed in Poland was reminiscent of the namespace spirit of a nation torn out of the ground.

Nevertheless, because many of the composers contributed to the cause of Polish nationalism, none was able to do so with the same sort of easy, instinctive naturalness with which Fryderyk Chopin was able to do so, beyond possibly being a virtuoso concert pianist. Chopin still to this day is considered the biggest Polish icon, piano composer and performer as well as one of the most outstanding figures in music history. Now millions know a man gifted and famous European-born composer Chopin whose music grew naturally out of Polish folk and was in its turn both consciously and unconsciously used as a medium of local patriotism.

Chopin was born in the era of partitions, and he grew up in Warsaw, which undoubtedly speaks about his direct contact with folk music. Despite the young Chopin's performing career and later working most of his career in Europe and specifically in France, his music reflected his Polish heritage in its entirety. He once wrote in a letter, 'I am a revolutionary, a Pole, willing to fight anyplace for our fatherland with the piano.' His mazurkas and polonaises contain the themes that are characteristic of traditional Polish dance tunes. These are those that may be sad or moody and bring out the Polish troubles but have glimmers of a pleasant resurrection.

Analyzing the character of Chopin's career, his critics would comment on how the artist had wanted to add some emotional tone to his music different from the remaining classical music in Europe. In 1843 the American music journal The Albion noted that all of Chopin's compositions "are Polish through and through, they are the music of Poland"). Still in France he was perceived as an oriental and a truly Polish musician was referred to as 'plus polonaise que le Polonais' and the 'poète de la Pologne'.

Chopin also referred to Polish nationalism to a greater extent at some points. This heroic Polonaise in A flat major (1831) for Piano entitled 'For Polish Cavalry' was composed for the Polish troops who were serving under the French. It opens with a rather pompous proclamation in the brass section recreating the style of the famous cavalrymen. This leads to a stately processional with those runs, and ornaments that may suggest images of the Polish Hussars marching or charging with spears.

Same with Chopin in his Polonaise in Ab Major op 53, the melody in the left hand is clearly vocalized and many historians opined that it is as if the music was sung by a woman. It sings out the plea: The phrase 'Poland is not yet lost,' would be the first line of the song that would later become the acclaimed Polish national anthem. Chopin's notes were better than mere notes as they depicted visions and went along with feelings and feelings intrinsically connected with the Polish character and fight.

As the phenomenon of Polish nationalism, the genius of Chopin touched the emotions and souls of people all over the globe with the least rhythm, dramatics and passion. The Mazureks became brilliant ballroom dance tunes not only in Europe but in America also later on. Every woman in the salons in Paris almost had a fainting spell with Chopin's good looks not to mention the soft touch of his piano playing. Newspapers exalted him as the star of the age, meaning more than a simply great continental virtuoso but one of the greatest musical prodigies on the same level as Mozart and Beethoven.

Thus, having performed and composed in foreign countries, and having found posthumous success, Chopin was also the first introduction to the Polish music and the Polish manner of feeling to the entire world. He prepared for other composers including

Karol Szymanowski, Witold Lutoslawski and other people to enhance global visibility of Polish styles existing at the change of the twentieth century. The Poles residing in various parts of the world also spread Chopin music to North and South America where Polish connection has always been valued.

To this very day, Chopin is considered not only a musician in his country but even a Polish deity of Poland and its sufferings. Fakes can be bought in every Warsaw shop that sells souvenirs: Chopin balls, mugs, paintings, and many other items. He has been depicted on the banknotes and the postal envelopes of Poland. All the greater part of Chopin's manuscripts are stored as national treasures in the Museum of Fryderyk Chopin in Warsaw. The States international of classical music returns again and again to Poland's international Chopin piano competition. Even though Fryderyk Chopin left this world a long time ago, he is still giving concerts as the maestro of the divided motherland and as the globally recognized representative of music and aesthetics for the ears of people all over the world.

In about the mid-1800s, polish composers started looking at how they could introduce facets of Polish folk music into their music. One such movement that began in Poland is referred to as the Polish Folk Revival, and this was among the trends whereby European composers began to introduce folk influences into their compositions.

The main causes of the politicization for the revival of Polish Folk Revival include the following. Poland had been partitioned between Russia, Prussia and Austria in the last decade of the eighteenth century and barred of nationality. The efforts toward the integration of facets of Polish folk into pieces were viewed as a way of expressing the emerging Polish nationalism since during that time there was no Polish state. Another factor that played a part was Romantic nationalism which meant that there was growing interest in Polish folk culture. The Polish composers and scholars endeavored to search for the primitive Polish folk tunes, airs and dances in the field for the basis of compositions.

The first trend that could be attributed to the concept of the Polish Folk Revival in music originated in the works of Maria Szymanowska (1789-1831), who was writing mazurkas for piano – a composition that combined the Polish and classical dances. Another composer who contributed to the development of the Polish folk style was

Chopin who wrote many mazurkas and polonaises for solo piano but under the nos of piano études.

Other later composers who were working to include the Polish folk in Polish classical music include Moniuszko (1819-1872) he used real Polish elements in his operas whereby he included genuine Polish elements in the melodies and rhythms of his songs. From his works, we can name the operas Halka and The Haunted Manor and both of them include dances and songs which are recollected with the Polish folk songs.

The Polish Folk Revival was also continued by the Young Poland movement of the end of the nineteenth century which concentrated on the Polish culture and art as the way to gain independence for Poland. Those Young

Poland composers as Mieczysław Karłowicz (1876–1909) created compositions in orchestra where they used the modal scales, drones, and rhythmic ostinato from the Highlander folk music. Masurkas with specific Polish folk features are featured mainly in the Episode at a Masquerade, a symphonic poem by Karłowicz.

Moreover, Polish composers who were writing at the beginning of the twentieth century also kept a harmonic of Polish music in their classical songs. Karol Szymanowski completed several compositions that depict influences of modernism with occasional polonist elements and these are Violin Concerto No. 1 and ballet Harnasie. Incorporating some of the music modalities and rhythms from the Polish Highlander, Harnasie uses folk, common practice, and modernist music to build a picture of a pagan past.

The Polish Folk Revival Movement did not only involve composers from within the geographical borders of Poland The non-Polish composers also incorporated some of the characteristics of the Polish Folk Music into their compositions. The Polish Christmas carol tune for instance, has been quoted by Russia's Nikolai Rimsky-Korsakov in the first movement of her Symphony No. 3 while several mazurkas by Russian composer Pyotr Ilyich Tchaikovsky, (1840-1893) are seen to have Chopin's influence and in general, Polish dance music. Thus, many personalities, who were not Polish, but included Polish folk motifs, contributed to bringing Polish Folk Revival stylistics all across Europe and the world.

Taking Polish music folklore into cantabile compositions was carried on to mid of the twentieth century by Witold Lutosławski 1913 – 1994, Krzysztof Penderecki 1933-, Henryk Górecki 1933-. Although the strict approach of Polish Folk Revival was dismantled by the early 1950s, the procedure of including aspects of Polish musical folklore in combination with modernist/postmodernist forms remained inherent to the 20th and the 21st centuries Polish composers. However, it is possible to find fugitives of Polish folk music in compositions of those contemporary composers who are alive at the present moment including Hanna Kulenty (born in 1943), Pawel Szymanski (born in the year 1954), Agata Zubel (born in 1978), etc. The historical linking of the two realized by the Polish Folk Revival is rather intriguing and links the past to the present of Polish music.

Apart from a kindling impact in the current analyzed Polish composers, as it has been presented and considered earlier, traditional Polish folk music has left stylistic traces in several other important late romantic and twentieth-century European composers in general.

Chopin was one of the ways that Polish folk music influenced the European classical music in their country. Fundamentals of Polish music as seen in Chopin's mazurkas polonaises and other piano works impacted many composers other than Poland.

For instance, Chopin's idiom was felt to have made a considerable impact on the other late/ Romantic piano composers known as

Johannes Brahms 1833–1897. Thus, the majority of piano works by Brahms contain direct quotations from Chopin, and also allusions to the kind of modality and dance that characterize Chopin's transformation of Polish folk music. In addition to direct borrowings, Chopin's pianistic style which is reminiscent of Polish folk music is also reflected in Some aspects of Brahms' melodies: the series of chords also known as harmonic progressions and accents or rhythmic feels.

For instance, the Czech composer of the Romantic era, Antonin Dvorak (1841 – 1904) was also guilty of using materials from Chopin among other Polish compatriots. Reference was made to opus 46 and 72, by Dvořák, which had a direct relation to Slavonic Dances and others that recalled the Spirit of the Czechs and Poles in Music in general of the

Slavic theme. More covertly, some of Dvořák's sonata and section vigorously contain Polish folk rhythm, mode and imitative melodic figures due to Chopin's influence and others.

Chopin and his later followers proved that Polish folk music was still alive and effective in composition, and did not wane with the next generations of music. Such historical developments of Chopin's Polish mazurka style can be referred to as Claude Debussy, Aleksandr Scriabin, Sergei Rachmaninoff and other composers. These composers slavishly copied Chopin's characteristic textural, harmonic, or rhythmic answers to Polish folk that inspired him and in so doing transformed Chopin's idiom into other spheres.

Indeed, certain Polish folk musical motifs have been integrated into the knowledge base of many avant-garde composers at the beginning of the 20th century thanks to pieces such as Szymanowski's Violin Concerto No. 1 and ballet Harnasie. In these pieces, apparent avant-garde techniques attracted the attention of international modernist composers.

Many composers of the so-called "neoclassical" period such as Igor Stravinsky, Maurice Ravel Paul Hindemith to mention but a few incorporated in their works imitations of Polish folk melodies, Polish modal scales, Polish complicated rhythms, and dissonant vertical harmonizations from Szymanowski or any other Polish composer. These composers were busy disseminating Polish folk music traits in their circles and networks by incorporating specifically Polish-inflected music in some of the most popular and 'globalized', cosmopolitan musical forms of the early twentieth century.

Thus in as many ways described above Polish folk music left its mark on the Polish national composers inspired by this genre as well as on the non-Polish composers who incorporated elements of Polish folk music into their compositions. That inspiration was the Polish folk material which in turn gave the imprint on European classical music on the concealed as well as on the manifest level during the mid-19th century until the early part of the 20th century. The spirit of various characteristics of Polish music is reflected in hundreds of performances of great masters of classical music: dance movements, modal scales, expressive melodies, and sharp harmonies that one can find in folk-oriented Polish music can be attributed to these enthusiasts.

Resilience and Innovation

The years between the two world wars in Poland which were 1918 – 1939 was also a significant period of social and political change that inflicted music in the nation. Poland was forging a new state after over a century of external occupation, even though the ethnopolitical tensions, economic recession and the consequent authoritarianism prevailed. It was such a climate which determined the trends Polish music followed in this era.

In the classical field, some of the composers like Karol Szymanowski began to develop a nationalist style that incorporated folk tunes of Poland and other developing contemporary styles that prevailed in the European Union. His other ballet Harnasie (1923) used Podhale highlander tunes, as well as rhythmic motifs associated with the Tatra Mountains and Impressionistic harmony. Let me mention other cases of other composers who chose different paths – neoclassicism for Grażyna Bacewicz's violin concertos, aleatory for Witold Lutosławski's first symphonies.

Politically, with the rise of a new extremism in the course of the 1930s, new music came into being. Essialists accused avant-garde musicians of depriving Poles of their culture because of their inclination toward abstract modernism. Szymanowski experienced the same thing through compositions such as

Symphony No. 3 aimed at synthesizing Polish traits in music with contemporary techniques. The same with official censorship, it also rose with the more disciplined authoritarianism of the Sanacja – one had to be careful not to introduce anything revolutionary to the composition.

Popular music also evolved in conjunction with the changes that were taking place in the society of Poland. The interwar period was an age of 'boom,' and especially for the germinating culture of urban, Warsaw and Krakow, in particular, were the night clubs, cafes, theaters, and cinemas nightlife. Another new industry of the recording industry of songs on the gramophone for sales to consumers.

Of them, the basisty and the kabarety have found a preferential place – musical-comedy theaters or satiric revue theaters. Some of the performers like Julian Tuwim and Marian Hemar were able to bring the cultural ethos to the stage through jazzy songs that were accompanied by funny political jokes on most of the social issues. Their songs were a rebellion against military authoritarianism and materialism – and the evidence immediately pointed to defiant streams that continued to exist although the process of censorship was getting bigger.

Penthouse offered some songs with such themes as hope and freedom while other songs provided themes such as imagination and dreaming. The serenades about love, but not a happy one, contributed to popularizing the poetessa, for instance, Mira Zimińska-Sygietyńska. They were touching songs that evolved into the representatives of the Polish popular song in the interwar period together with the basisty satires.

All of the strains demonstrated the relationship between the musical tradition of Poles and politics as well as social attitudes throughout the period of instability. It should only be noted that the songs and compositions were made since the time when there was turmoil – in response to them or as a respite from them.

The War started on September 1st in the year 1939 when Germany attacked Poland; the flame of culture that had been burning for many years was put off and the people suffered for five years of occupation. The rich musical life of the interwar period - the concert composers borrowing tunes from the folk and the eccentric, the singers and the bands of the cabaret performing their working-class ironic songs, the poetessas who were singing their lover's songs - all of them ended with the approach of the second world war in Europe.

As one would expect from two hostile totalitarian regimes, the Nazis and the Soviets tried to stamp out Polish music, but they were not entirely successful. The poles also danced and sang covertly and even in such circumstances they demonstrated the sustainability of Polish culture when there was very bad persecution. Secreted folk song archives, covert composition, and music-making in the ghettos and camps as well as under occupation: the period of Occupation, in my opinion, revealed both the greatest pain as well as the ability to create something out of it.

The first ones to feel the pinch were the musical organizations – closed conservatories, disbanded orchestras and shut down publishing houses. Several cities of Poland including Warsaw were under fire and occupied by Germans which reduced the colourful Polish culture. Avant-garde music from modernist composers and playwrights was never easy because their works were banned as 'substandard' examples of degenerate modernism. Vitacims were Lutosławski's mentor and father-in-law who both were murdered in the mass killings.

However, as all the pessimists had predicted, music did not die out in the early years of the war. With the feeling they were being pushed, did not ignore lessons and training even though most music schools were shut. In some circumstances, sneak performances were given, thereby offending the Germans who had already banned Polish art on their soil The most talented of the singers and dancers found themselves barely able to scrape a living from performances in cafes and restaurants, and continued the traditions of song and dance in the night world, living in fear of their suppressors.

However, organized resistance will be documented in other forms of culture and through education in the future. There were also hidden schools, like the Flying University in Warsaw or the University of Western Lands in Lvov where Polish music could carry on even when the Nazis tried to eliminate it. Choirs in occupied Poznan were singing guerrilla songs; they published booklets with patriotic songs so that people could make themselves feel better and also keep their traditions.

Another way that musical resilience and resistance could be preserved was through folk culture and this would mostly apply to the Polish countryside. Polish ethnomusicologist Jadwiga Sobieska was nearly killed while collecting the Highlander melodies in the villages of the Tatra Mountain over three hundred of these tunes are documented today. Likewise, other field researchers endeavored to record folk music from occupied territories since the countryside preserved the spirit of the nation.

Jewish ghettos mostly experienced the strongest form of musical defiance by the Polish people. While starvation enveloped artists and musicians in the ubications of Warsaw, Krakow and other cities, they undertook quite extraordinary performances, ranging from symphony orchestras, jazz bands, theatre groups, cabaret acts and music schools for children. Thus, music became the people's way of fighting existentialism with a violinist or a young suffragette singing protest songs against deportation to extermination camps through chorality. Lyrical and touching songs always sing a story where there is a fall, and then the ever-rising and rising against all odds stories.

And it is possible to mention that some of the Nazi camps also turned into places of radical musical activity. The prisoners in Auschwitz were compelled to play music in the orchestras and bands for their captors — but at night they wrote their songs, using their captors' tools and instruments they had been able to seize, with captured symbols. It was also possible to contemplate survival, improving prisoner care, or even swapping shifts through songs. However, the female prisoners were even more rebellious transforming from writing heartfelt folk songs to composing the opera about the horrors of the camp. Though most musicians were assassinated through gas chambers people were given moral nourishment through culture and rebellion.

Worse came with the Occupation during the Occupation years, Poland received the worst through loss and suffering that can hardly be measured. But it also has revealed how strong music was – no matter whether ethnomusicologists, documenting given peoples cultures, ghetto musicians, offering hope or prisoners using songs as a form of spiritual rebellion. It was a history of a world that was capable of horrendous suffering, but also one which refused to be extinguished, a political testament to the hate of fascist regimes. Such enthusiastic musical ties made it possible to preserve Polish culture during the worst scenario before revival could be possible in the post-war period.

Nevertheless, Polish culture was lively in between the war period and war-ravaged Poland experienced a rapid rise in culture in the post-war era. It was here however in the arts that a nation was reborn not just the society and the economy. This restoration of the dynamism of Poles was done during the mid-20th century music through cinema and mass media. The dynamic soundtracks and new approaches towards songwriting given to Polish music in the post-war phases gave it an essential place in the new voice of the nation after the war years.

The most peculiar period was called the 'golden age' and it referred to the Polish film music that developed from the middle of the fifties till the beginning of the sixties. With the new generation of composers, the cinematic narrative was further improved from the works which greater liberators like Andrzej Wajda brought back the country's movie-making when German and Soviet invaders left the place.

The avant-rock fusionist Krzysztof Komeda was best at providing jazzy tunes for Wajda's war films as well as the films related to trauma and the dreamlike sixties' parable. Renowned classicist Tadeusz Baird included operatic timbre as a descriptor of adventure such as Knights of the Teutonic Order by brass and drums. As for the and experimental one, Zygmunt Konieczny disrupted and honed cuts for the surreal/psychological horror ones.

As distinctive for these films were the vocal themes created in collaboration with these films – romantic hits like the ballad "Lonely Street" by Roman Palester or "Last Day of Summer" by Konieczny which was played by radio all over the country. Whether it is about rich scores or burning lyrics, the Polish cinema demonstrated the reborn artistry to be the direct outcome of conflict's dismissal of art.

The radio sphere also offered the chance of renewal in the music and the procedure of experimenting for the nation as technology developed. Thus, Polish Radio which had been the state enterprise at that time on one had collected records and ethnographic outputs to retell folk traditions and, on the other, had encouraged talent among young people.

Consequently, the music of avant-garde that includes Penderecki and Lutoslawski comes into the domain of the majority of the population with the radio playback of their abstract experimentation with the orchestras. By the beginning of the sixties, Luxtion Records listed in the Polish chronicles of the electric rock and electronic music from throughout the Eastern Bloc to distribute vinyl records.

The stage also benefited the course of music by supporting annual festivals like the Warsaw Autumn which had been established to prevent Stalinist oppression however later it promoted domestic sonic discovery and foreign avant-gardes which included

Stockhausen and Xenakis. Two other Polish composers raised in the domestic tradition Górecki and Szalonek also followed the trend of progressing ever-liberated modernism.

When Poland was occupied in 1944 the new authorities quickly started to take control over the music production. The state then learned that music was a powerful instrument for the propagation of communism. For this reason, after World War II Poland's government built a huge number of organizations and bureaucracies to control music and possibly provide censorship over it. The Ministry of Culture and Art was the conductor of education; however, different agencies like, the Polish Composers Union exposed a widespread state authority.

The most pressing need was to create music that would glorify communism in word and deed. The authorities of Poland demanded triumphalist art – the art that would celebrate Joseph Stalin and other Soviet leaders. The state composers composed marches, oratorios, and symphonies about the suffering of the proletariat and dreaming of communism's success. The regime felt that certain musicians and music groups should be given adequate state remunerations and benefits with the condition that they should continue to produce politically correct music.

For example, there was the state control of the large songs and dance ensemble Mazowsze, which presented basic musical folklore, relevant to the state ideals and adjusted if necessary. Some of these were state-sanctioned songs that were played on Polish radio to reach a larger populace with the message being passed on. Furthermore, the government of Poland sought to make the music monotonous and conformist by decentralizing the portfolios and subjugating artists for communism, thus coming up with cheerleading music that upheld communism.

But to invent the superstructure of this callous musically propagandistic exterior was only one strategy the state had in mind. More profoundly, Poland's leaders wanted to achieve the omni-interpretation of the role of music in society about communism and gain consent for and stability in the process. It presupposed intensive censoring of the works that could be deemed dangerous or rebellious and at the same time active promotion of the official cultural policy.

The regime brought censorship and musicians and composers before they could perform any piece of music had to get permission from the state censors. Regarding analysis of the lyrical content and other elements of the tunes including harmony, rhythms and so on, the officials wanted to know if they came with 'no negation of socialist?' However, after censorship, the regime ensured that the same music got good working through music criticism.

For instance, rather than the complete prohibition of compositions, officials tend to call for alterations of sections deemed obscene or subversive. This complicated process allowed the state to regulate music in a way that did not provoke a reaction that too brute force methods can sometimes stir up. This system of name-calling for patronage was repellent to most musicians as they had no other option other than to play this game to make their careers and create good music.

But, as censorship helped to create the new Musically cultured communist society the line was blurred and regulated only with the permission of party leaders. Now, state censors have forbidden all songs that touch the subject of Polish nationalism in any way implying rejection of communism and internationalism. In the same manner, the means of dissonance and atonality that are considered the formalist methods were admissible to represent moral degradation.

Hymns and Christmas singing were named as obstacles of the regime coming from the sphere of the bourgeois culture. It was still forbidden to commemorate the freedom movements like the monument of the Warsaw

Uprising as they provoked too much pre-communist nationalism. In this control apparatus, the state brought in taboos and muffled the tunes that went against the happy party line.

Thus, choosing several strategies in their relations between compromised collaboration and defiance, musicians in Poland. Thus, for many, concessions were already the only possible way to maintain the intensity of the artistic process to pressure from the sides of the parties' oversight. Other composers like Witold Lutoslawski and Krzysztof Penderecki made efforts to expand the borders to progress Polish music by the constraints available to them. It also came up with yummy state-approved pieces like Lutoslawski's Concerto for Orchestra as well as risky abstractions.

Without turning into rebellion with revolutionary tendencies they nevertheless overextended the frame of free speech by augmenting the Polish musical tape. Other artists like Serocki for example went to folklore with its clear reference to the national culture, but like everybody else in the 1950s and 1960s, he did so under the guise of socialist realism. Thus, within limitations, the musicians subtilely choreographed their specific actions to convey a hidden message using space.

However, increased resistance against 'Yuan Li' also resulted in confrontation as well. Some of the composers grumbled about political education sessions; radical students did not turn up for lectures on the Marxist approach. If they failed to perform politically affiliated songs including anthems, state musicians were sacked; especially after Stalin was denounced in 1956 which assumes the Soviet purge presumed communists.

And such genres as jazz, for example, immediately adopted those Western trends and became one of the genres that were a part and parcel of the underground culture which existed owing to the uncontrolled infrastructural growth. Thus, latent tension between the minority musicians and the intrusive state control were expressed as oppositional poses to violate artistic freedom.

The aim of tightening and easing the control in Poland by the communist authority was to erect a thought-out network of supervision to subdue the music for ideological domination. It is within this context that most of the repertoire created from 1944-1989 can be said to be highly politicized. However, by also developing one more superficial layer of health, the state musical policy was, at the very best, utterly ineffectual regarding the implanted goals of deep absorption while, at the very worst, it created generations of artistic animosity toward it.

As for communism, the pressure from outside facilitated its gradual disintegration throughout Europe by 1989 and similarly inside the Polish musical life there was observed both interaction and conflict which led to a period of renewed freedom to be more expressive.

Its fall started immediate liberation for Polish music as state censorship which for several decades had dominated the Polish music scene evaporated almost instantaneously. There is one more aspect: religion, Polish identity, Western influences and other topics that would have been forbidden and censored in the past could be depicted within art by artists without restrictions. If before new styles were expected to conform to bureaucratic taste and appearance of objects, it was no longer the case.

Finally, they also had not been passive and having gone through severe critical reviews, composers were happy to dismiss the remains of socialist relations and start their practice. Poland changed political systems and had become a pluralistic democracy by 1992. The joy, the freedom and most of all the membership in a global market economy started an extraordinary renaissance of Polish music on an extraordinary scale throughout.

However, with political transformation came diminishing state support and emergent potent economic concerns. Musicians, as well as all those involved in the production of music, had to depend on private organizations such as the Polish Music Publishers Forum to organize for financial support. With few successful being able to gain commercial self-employment, many also had to resort to teaching or competition such as the Witold Lutoslawski Award for young composers.

Nonetheless, the extent of the subsequent post-communist musical evolution did not only remained extensive but was also noticeably diverse, indicating the range of directions previously open to creators which earlier had been restrained. A great deal of activity focused on modernist styles. On his part, Lutoslawski himself went on developing his avant-garde language throughout the generation of his death in 1994.

Similarly, other young innovators such as Krzysztof Knittel and Hanna Kulenty created disjointed and experiments. Moreover, such global tendencies as minimalism and electronic music influenced Polish concert music through such a personality as Aleksander Lasoń. Yet, traditional genres were also revived with vigor including sacred music from the Gregorian chants to the religious opera like Pawel Mykietyn's staged Pascha.

Folk music also saw a revival for its ability to celebrate Polish identity and for its profitability. Thanks to festivals, films as well as concerts and recordings with world music artists, folk ensembles such as Mazowsze and Śląsk started receiving virtually unprecedented exposure. When performers ventured into the realms of popular music, bands and singers composed and sang traditional hymns and dances to techno music.

By the incorporation of folk tunes banned under communism, artists reinforced the cultural element aurally as Poland established a national course.

The early post-communist years also fostered Poland's modern pop and rock scene as well. When the state stepped aside and let record companies compete for the rights to distribute new bands, new independent labels emerged. Emerging trends such as the big beat, punk, grunge and heavy metal bands imported western rock music.

But Polish lyrics also made sure that new musical imports would be related to the special sociopolitical situation. The punk cabaret singer named as Kazik Staszewski enthusiastically offended the post-soviet mentality and called the modern change. Similarly, the rock band Lady Pank mythologized the politics of political visionaries by encapsulating the political instinct in such tracks as "The Prophet" as well as the belief in democracy.

By the late 1990s the locally grown styles got a foreign touch through the perspectives of the imported styles where the locally developed recording industry boomed into exporting products such as the death metal group Behemoth.

The superabundance of creativity that appeared after 1989 years indicates that there was potential before, albeit it was restrained by communism. Between such values as censorship and democratic freedom, Polish music enriched the catalog beyond the ideology and returned a cultural value to it. The numerous directions of current output made modern output return to the traditional Polish musical orientations and, at the same time, introduce components of the styles identified by the new global soundscape.

Ranging from avant-rock fusions to neo-traditionalist ensembles, the plethora of changes itself directly to the country's post-communist configurational rebirth in sound. As the source of propaganda, it has now resulted in the phenomenon of the current Polish music as both asserting the national culture and contributing to the world culture as it is in the contemporary changes of geopolitical systems. Hence, with infinite new timbres, Lau's free at-last expression now coming through must mean even more doors opening musically in the future.

Future Directions

Poland has always had a musical culture that goes back centuries with compositions and folk songs that depict the history of Poland. Poland's integration into the global society and the digital age has impacted the direction of contemporary Polish music in the past few decades.

Despite current Polish artists trying to maintain their cultural identity, they have incorporated various modern music styles such as hip-hop, electronic and pop into their songs. The mixing of the existing Polish rhythms such as mazurka with modern rhythms produces an interesting mix that people today find appealing.

One of the genres that have grown to an international level is Polish hip hop. O.S.T.R., Pezet, and Sokół are the artists whose work can be classified as Polish hip hop that originated from American rap but has its unique sound – Polish lyrics over both hip hop and EDM instrumental. With their songs about life in today's Poland, they have managed to tour Europe and beyond.

Singer Brodka as well as an alternative rock band named Hey are also contributing to Polish indie music entering the international market since their songs are mostly in English. Their musical style is experimental and postmodern which reflects Poland as an urban and multicultural country today. However, they occasionally use Polish culture and historical references to express themselves.

With Polish music penetrating even more global markets, musicians get more opportunities to incorporate aspects of other cultures into new Polonized sounds that intensify Polish voices. The combination of musical flows coming from different parts of the world might bring exciting new perspectives to polish contemporary music.

Polish folklore and traditional music play an important role in the cultural development of Poland throughout the centuries. Being contemporary artists many of them incorporate traditional Polish motifs into modern genres. These combined sounds, as we see, are the way, on the one hand, to keep the tradition alive and, on the other, to transform it into new trends.

Today, the most famous one in the sphere of popular music and known as the combination of Polish folk songs with Pop music, the band Tulia sings more modern covers of the classics. Their first single, 'Jeszcze Cię Nie Ma' is a folk-pop song that influences a traditional Polish lullaby, though it is embellished with some synthesizers that are pop.

Otsochodzi, a Polish rapper has the ability to sample mazurkas or polka and then turn it into fast rap beats. Żywiołak seems to be folk, and it is a trio consisting of folk and village musicians and reggae and ska musicians. The folk derivative inherent in the sounds of the hybrid is a reference to tradition, while the direction of Polish music development is opened.

Apart from the pop spheres, similar tendencies are incorporated into the Polish representatives of classical music concerning folk and modern tendencies. Some of those using a fusion of jazz and folk songs are Anna Maria Jopek-singer, Resina-a cellist and the Lautari Quartet.

It also presented the works of a mix of the traditional orchestral, electronic and folk artists which represents both the has-beens and the up-and-coming through the Witold Lutosławski Contemporary Music Forum. The only thing that can be said at this point is that as the software continues to advance and as ethnomusicological archives become available then there is always the potential for creating more refined hybrids.

Because of embracing the folklore and efforts to translate it into contemporary compositions, musicians of Polish origin regardless of the style and genre, are blending folklore with avant-garde. That is why musical personalities' hybrids, such as, for example, are filled with extraordinary passion for Polish culture. Such a musical evolution appears to be an effort that will ensure that the values of the culture are taught to future generations.

Polish folklore has remained an art that was practically narrated from one generation to another in small groups among the Polish people for many centuries. This is because, stories, songs and tales were Informational inventions, reflecting history, values and wisdom. However, industrialization and globalization have skewed the shape of sustainable patterns. With the change of cultures comes a change in lifestyles which is a threat to cultural heritage.

Digital technologies now have a significant role in the preservation of endangered Polish folklore by offering broader ways to collect, share and send people back to their origins. Ethnomusicology archives remain energetically active in the process of documenting vanishing village songs as the generation still possessing the living memory of the old tunes is gradually dying out.

Online universities such as the University of Warsaw have vast databases for folk music from remote areas of the world. There are such initiatives like "Traditional Music in

Poland" where users can upload the folk music heard in village fairs by sharing the existing sites and smartphones. These tapes thus document a form of singing that is on the verge of disappearing. Organized, easily searchable databases allow academic researchers and casual listeners alike to find rural sounds that may otherwise disappear.

Geographical databases such as the National Geographic Information System in Poland combine sites associated with cultural history or mythology with folklore or legends by mapping areas of a village, castle, or nature conservation area with related sites. Engaging with these visual cultural archives can assist the new generations, raised in cities, to reestablish proximities with disrupted relations with Poland's living folklore geographies and pasts.

Culture ministries fund video projects that showcase elderly village musicians singing folk songs in homes, thereby preserving not only tunes, but also traditions, dances, and recipes, and the final echoes of a worldview. However, in the form of videos, elders' experiences remain conspicuous and evocative of indigenous culture. Augmented and virtual reality technologies assist in the representation of the old Polish village existence.

In this manner, mass digitization safeguards the cultural memory of the Polish people and lends a new lease of life to it through technology. In this way, it enables traditions proceeding from rural communities for a thousand years to resound in the modern epoch, giving new generations knowledge and serving as an example.

Interestingly music in the digital media has grown everywhere and democratized the control of popular culture sound. As for Polish music compositions, the further evolution of new tendencies in the direction of folk and popular music directions within the context of an interactive multimedia environment is almost infinite. Today, thanks to streaming services, social networks, and relatively cheap mixing platforms, new independent musicians are capable of creating new music connected with Polish identity that can travel around the world.

Both YouTube and Spotify contributed a lot to the acceleration of the speed of entry to the market for novice musicians from Poland and allowed them to place their compositions within the framework of the greatest hits of large record companies. Some of these channels which include POLSKA TOP 10 play pop playlists for the youthful population. More recent compilations, such as "Polska" and "Piano Bar", offer a frequently changing list of artists that are presented from indie rock to mainstream pop artists, originating from folk music.

Companion to the streaming platforms, the production instruments assist the new artists to achieve what would represent the Polish experience in the songs. Some of the genuine traditional country singers who previously could not directly connect with everyone now make simple homemade music videos.

T.V talent competitions also played a role in creating awareness of folk and traditional music because talents also sing both village songs and popular songs. The access to media has greatly amplified the rudimentary involvement of the public in Polish legacy.

From folklore to the stage, folk music has become the new TikTok trend to sample the "Oh No" song over the Mazurka. Such Folktronica bands as Bubliczki profit from doing so since these samples are fitted into identifiable EDM tracks that can be uploaded to streaming services. You see, tradition overall alters when social media becomes involved and becomes global new remixes.

At the national level, it has been identified that the Polish government has made certain efforts in the safeguarding of intangible cultural heritage. UNESCO, as a global organization, is concerned with Poland's folk culture yet it has categorized the Krakovanka and Mazurka dances, the tradition of bagpipe, the paper cutting of the Nativity scene, as well as several religious song repertoires under its endangered list. Poland has risen to the challenge of eradicating these practices and where they have been practiced they should not be passed down orally from one generation to another but rather through schools for children to practice them and continue from there.

Polish countryside also contains many diversified museums of architecture where one can see what Polish villages looked like in the past, as well as the peasant costumes, ornamentation and traditions. The first one and the most important one is the Museum of Folk Architecture in Sanok which consists of over 150 wooden buildings and contains a collection of folk artefacts for all regions of Poland, numbering over 300000 pieces. Such preservation allows the guests of the historic site to have a firsthand experience of the village life as was in the 19th and 20th centuries.

This would go hand in hand with elements such as music, from that of the concertos of Frederic Chopin to the Harvest Fair songs. With a view of competing with the tops in the charts of pop music Radio Poland has established a station termed as Poland Folk Radio that plays folk traditional and modern music continuously to popularize the Genrë. Another official event is Wrocław's Wratislavia Cantans festival which promotes itself as having given performances ranging from medieval European chants to contemporary Polish folktronica. A sort of respect for the old as well as the new is typical of the Polish preservation process.

But cultural conservation in Poland is not only in large-scale institutional Initiatives; artists and those who are into practices at the ground level are also involved. When the arts of wycinanki were depreciating, ordinary people decided to form wycinanki circles in the villages they lived in. These local masters transmit it to the learners so that they can have traditional cut paper motifs incorporated into the contemporary graphic art, costumes as well as set props. Consequently, everyday amateur dance ensembles as well as folk choirs throughout Poland still practice and perform regional songs and dances from centuries ago with first original choreography and second with often original instrumentation. This participatory spirit involves the preservation of heritage as an art form that is dynamic and going through various evolutions based on the present trends.

Slightly younger Polish musicians are also now reinterpreting Folk music by adding electronic music elements. Accompanied by technology help, Warsaw Village Band and Kapela Maliszów ensembles play bagpipe songs and string sections as well as dance rhythms. Their albums get into the top ten within short periods in Poland; this gives a clue that the youth is willing to embrace change in many other ramifications of cultural traditions. Thus, folk culture remains important where such new genres are concerned.

Another active member of Kapela Maliszów, Janusz Prusinowski was also involved in putting into drive the folk revival campaign in

Poland through a project known as Naviband. to go and collect folk songs anywhere in the country including the villages. They capture the songs on the move using documentary videos on the channel, and they have elderly persons playing music, which has been passed from one generation to another. It makes it possible to record threatened songs to be preserved for future generations while at the same time letting the youth know that such practices are performing arts. Short documentaries are one of the ways to build on cultural sustainability from the past to the present.

A village that best illustrates the effectiveness of preservation and innovation is Zalipie, which has been involved in the artistic craft for 900 years During this period, women in the village paint cottages with floral designs. This painstaking craft gradually became extinct by the 1960s until the village reinvented itself as Poland's folkloric open-air painting museum. Thus, today Zalipie has become a cultural tourism site where thousands of tourists attend workshops, paint cottages with modern interpretations of folk motifs, and buy folk crafts that are made to support the restoration of historical buildings. Returning to life as a living museum, Zalipie preserves an artistic tradition dear to Poland's identity which was nearly lost in the past years.

As threatened were the exquisite paper-cutting artworks of wycinanki and komask making originated from the Kurpie region of Poland. These crafts were revived by the Szewczyk sisters, who are three artists who promoted their scissor work as cultural emissaries. They conducted workshops all over the world and recolored the old motifs of papercutting into graphics of apparel and outstanding modern art installations that are showcased from the Paris fashion ramps to the Australian museums. Their creativity thus proves how traditional folk elements can be fostered in contemporary media when one's individuality is nurtured. This is why Polish heritage lives on through artisans like the Szewczyks, who pay tribute to fantastic legends of the past while also breaking new grounds, and does not stagnate in tradition.

Polish folk string bands' arched basses have also been rewarded to masters like Witold Oleszak. This famous highlander's fiddler is very interested in the music of Podhale highlanders and spends much time researching and playing the music of an enclosed group of mountain dwellers- Podhale highlanders whose tunes are believed to be as pre-slavs as possible. When keeping the intonations of centuries, Oleszak conceived the first five-stringed electric bass which replicated the sound of the acoustic bass. His group called Trebunie Tutki combines electronic music with highlander pipes and zhalters resembling harps for such songs that present shepherds driving their cattle with bass beats in the background. How Witold was able to 'screw' the instruments into a socket of ancient folk songs that would conform to new contexts of performing was the best exemplification of the essences of both traditions and pliancy.

These measures together with the initiatives of artists, activists, governmental programs, cultural institutions and communities also make sure that Polish traditions relate to the past and are relevant to the present at the same time. Thus, initiating grassroots creative action as well as outreach encourages people to volunteer to disseminate the heritage their predecessors bequeathed. It is more of a living tradition and not something that you put in a museum and preserve for generations.

However, there are still some problems concerning the sustaining of folk arts in Poland as the governmental support is inconsistent. Another opposition is between cosmopolitised youth entertained by Anglophone music and media products and rural youths who were socialized to follow the family culture of their parents and actively participate in such ethnographically-laden events as Wianki. Maintenance of the work would mean raising cultural consciousness in all layers of the Polish population.

Nevertheless, the constant attempts to preserve culture point out the fact that Polish culture does not bow down to its defeat by stagnation even in the face of globalization. From the middle-aged bagpipe anthems to the communism era heroic ballads to the migrant worker songs each of these periods has their fair share in making up the rich musical tradition of Poland. Thus Polish people have managed to maintain what they originated from while making culture relevant in the sense of continuing it for each generation. If the deserves of the general public, creativity as well as experiment and institutional support are properly encouraged, then tradition and innovation may complement each other. This is the reason why cultural sustainability is possible.

As pointed out earlier, the living heritage is never devoid of its sources of replenishment from the mouth of the well of history – concerning the 'Polish Spring' that has been revealed in the dynamic forms of preservation.

For it has made hope for all the sacral creative traditions of mankind, which are threatened in the rapidly developing world of today. While, on the one side, culture still aims at the community identity as it grows beyond its confines in the search for novel concepts, and ideas, on the other side, collective memory remains impenetrable and resilient to being eroded through the ages. The Polish efforts of trying to achieve a work in progress along with preventive measures of conservation ensure that the world's cultural heritage is preserved for future use.

Disclaimer

Everything shared in this book should be considered as educational and informative in nature. The author and publisher shall not be responsible for any loss or damage suffered by any reader directly or indirectly through reading of, reliance on, and use of information that only the author and the publisher know at the time of writing this book.

Some of the suggestions given and the approaches recommended in the book may not be applicable to certain circumstances. The author and the publisher shall not be held responsible for any damages caused as a direct result of the use or non-use of the information presented in this book.

It is understood that readers should not rely on it for professional solicitations such as medical, legal, financial, and other related opinions. If any professional help is needed, then advice of a competent professional person should be taken.

The author and the publisher will not be held responsible for direct, indirect, special, or consequential damages or any other costs whatsoever arising from the use of the information present herein in this book.

About the Author

Maher Asaad Baker (In Arabic: ماهر أسعد بكر), is a Syrian musician, author, journalist, VFX & graphic artist, and director. He was born in Damascus in 1977. He grew up with a dream of being one of the most well-known artists in the world, and he has been working hard to achieve it ever since.

He started his career in 1997 when he was only 20 years old. He had a passion for technology and media, and he taught himself how to develop applications and websites. He also explored various types of media-creating paths, such as music production, graphic design, video editing, animation, and filmmaking. He was not satisfied with just being a consumer of media; he wanted to be a creator of media.

Reading was another source of inspiration for him. He was always surrounded by books as a child, thanks to his father's extensive library. He read books from different genres, topics, and perspectives. He read books for knowledge, for wisdom, for entertainment, for enlightenment. Reading stimulated his imagination and curiosity. Reading also developed his writing skills.

He did not start writing professionally until later in his life, as he was busy with other projects and pursuits. But when he did start writing, he proved himself to be a talented and prolific writer. He wrote articles for various newspapers and magazines on topics such as politics, culture, society, art, technology, and more. He wrote books that were informative and insightful. He wrote books that were creative and captivating. He wrote books that were best-selling and award-winning.

He is most known for his book "How I wrote a million Wikipedia articles", where he shares his experience of being one of the most prolific contributors to the online encyclopedia. He reveals his methods, techniques, strategies, and secrets of writing high-quality articles on any subject in record time. He also discusses the benefits and challenges of being a Wikipedia editor in the age of information overload.

He is also known for his novel "Becoming the man", where he tells the story of a young man who goes through a series of transformations in his life. The novel explores themes such as identity, masculinity, self-discovery, love, loss, and redemption. The novel is based on his journey to becoming who he is today.

Copyright © 2024 Maher Asaad Baker